ROBBINS LIBRARY, ARLINGTON, MASSACHUSETTS

W9-DDJ-182

"**Beautifully wrought and very moving. . . .
Horton Foote is an American original.**"
—*Variety*

"He's so quiet we have to slow down to hear him,
and then what he says is not so much surprising as
confirming. . . . I still believe every syllable of
Horton Foote, and envy him. He doesn't know how
to lie."　　　—John Leonard, *New York* magazine

"Impeccably wrought . . . A quietly elegant work
offering stages of ambiguity and depths."
—*Savannah News Press*

"A rich accumulation of textures."
—Jan Stuart, *Newsday*

**HORTON FOOTE** had his first Broadway play, *Only the
Heart*, produced in 1944. Today he remains a practicing
playwright dividing his talent between theater and film.
One of his best-known works is *The Trip to Bountiful*,
performed first on television in 1953, then produced as a
Broadway play, and finally filmed in 1985. Foote won his
first screenwriting Oscar for *To Kill a Mockingbird* in
1962 and his second for *Tender Mercies* in 1983. His
highly acclaimed nine-play cycle called *The Orphan's
Home* included *Roots in a Parched Ground*, *Lily Dale*,
and *Cousins*. His other recently produced plays are
*Taking Pictures*, *Night Seasons*, and *Laura Dennis*.

# THE
# YOUNG MAN
# FROM
#  ATLANTA

## HORTON FOOTE

A PLUME BOOK

AER-3335

812.54
FOO

PLUME
Published by the Penguin Group
Penguin Books USA Inc., 375 Hudson Street,
New York, New York 10014, U.S.A.
Penguin Books Ltd, 27 Wrights Lane, London W8 5TZ, England
Penguin Books Australia Ltd, Ringwood, Victoria, Australia
Penguin Books Canada Ltd, 10 Alcorn Avenue,
Toronto, Ontario, Canada M4V 3B2
Penguin Books (N.Z.) Ltd, 182–190 Wairau Road,
Auckland 10, New Zealand

Penguin Books Ltd, Registered Offices: Harmondsworth, Middlesex, England

Published by Plume, an imprint of Dutton Signet,
a division of Penguin Books USA Inc.
Previously published in a Dutton edition.

First Plume Printing, September, 1996
10 9 8 7 6 5 4 3 2 1

Copyright © Sunday Rock Corp., 1995
This work was first published in *American Theater*.

CAUTION: Professionals and amateurs are hereby warned that *The Young Man from Atlanta* is subject to a royalty. It is fully protected under the copyright laws of the United States of America, and of all countries covered by the International Copyright Union (including the Dominion of Canada and the rest of the British Commonwealth), and of all countries covered by the Pan-American Copyright Convention and the Universal Copyright Convention, and of all countries with which the United States has reciprocal copyright relations. All rights, including professional, amateur, motion picture, recitation, lecturing, public reading, radio broadcasting, television, video or sound taping, all other forms of mechanical or electronic reproduction, such as information storage and retrieval systems and photocopying, and the rights of translation into foreign languages, are strictly reserved. Particular emphasis is laid upon the question of readings, permission for which must be secured from the author's agent in writing.

The stage performance rights in *The Young Man from Atlanta* (other than first class rights) are controlled exclusively by the Dramatists Play Service, Inc., 440 Park Avenue South, New York, New York 10016. No professional or nonprofessional performance of the play (excluding first class professional performance) may be given without obtaining in advance the written permission of the Dramatists Play Service, Inc., and paying the requisite fee.

Inquiries concerning all other rights should be addressed to Barbara Hogenson, c/o The Barbara Hogenson Agency, Inc., 19 West 44th Street, Suite 1000, New York, New York 10036.

## SPECIAL NOTE

All groups receiving permission to produce *The Young Man from Atlanta* are required to (1) give credit to the author as sole and exclusive author of the play in all programs distributed in connection with performances of the play and in all instances in which the title of the play appears for purposes of advertising, publicizing or otherwise exploiting the play and/or a production thereof; the name of the author must appear on a separate line, in which no other name appears, immediately beneath the title and in size of type equal to 50 percent of the largest letter used for the title of the play. No person, firm or entity may receive credit larger or more prominent than that accorded the author and (2) To give the following acknowledgment on the title page in all programs distributed in connection with performances of the play:

"World premiere originally produced by Signature Theatre Company, James Houghton, Artistic Director, Thomas C. Proehl, Managing Director"

 REGISTERED TRADEMARK—MARCA REGISTRADA

The Library of Congress has catalogued the Dutton edition as follows:

Foote, Horton.
The young man from atlanta / Horton Foote.
p.    cm.
ISBN 0-525-94114-2 (hc.)
ISBN 0-452-27633-0 (pbk.)
1. Married people—Texas—Houston—Fiction.   2. Adult children—Death—Drama.   3. Loss (Psychology)—Drama.   4. Gay men—Drama.
I. Title.
PS3511.0344Y6   1995

812'.54—dc20

95-34479
CIP

Printed in the United States of America
Set in Century Light

## PUBLISHER'S NOTE

This is a work of fiction. Names, characters, places, and incidents either are the products of the author's imagination or are used fictitiously, and any resemblance to actual persons, living or dead, events, or locales is entirely coincidental.

Without limiting the rights under copyright reserved above, no part of this publication may be reproduced, stored in or introduced into a retrieval system, or transmitted, in any form, or by any means (electronic, mechanical, photocopying, recording, or otherwise), without the prior written permission of both the copyright owner and the above publisher of this book.

BOOKS ARE AVAILABLE AT QUANTITY DISCOUNTS WHEN USED TO PROMOTE PRODUCTS OR SERVICES. FOR INFORMATION PLEASE WRITE TO PREMIUM MARKETING DIVISION, PENGUIN BOOKS USA INC., 375 HUDSON STREET, NEW YORK, NY 10014.

*For Lillian*

# INTRODUCTION

Early in 1993, Jim Houghton approached me about the Signature Theatre doing a season of four of my plays. We had discussed this during their first season, when they were producing the plays of Romulus Linney, but I wasn't sure then that I was ready for such scrutiny.

I was out of New York the next season, when they did Lee Blessing's plays, but I was again in the city for the Edward Albee plays given in their third season. I was able to see most of these, and I was again very impressed by the theatre's work. So when Jim Houghton approached me once again, I decided to take the plunge. And, I might add, I'm mighty glad I did.

Both Romulus and Edward had elected to include plays of theirs that had been performed before in New York, as well as ones new to the city.

I decided to do all plays never before seen in New York. Two of them, *The Young Man from Atlanta* and *Laura Dennis*, were given first productions.

It was a busy time for this playwright, because I was encouraged to be present at all casting sessions, to go to rehearsals, and to attend as many performances as I could. I've never seen months go by quite so fast.

Signature decided to open the season with *Talking Pictures*, directed by Carol Goodheart. *Night Seasons*, which I directed, with a cast that included Jean Stapleton and Hallie Foote, followed. We took a break during the Christmas season, returning in late December to cast and rehearse *The Young Man from Atlanta*. Pete Masterson was to direct, and soon we had the casting all in place except for the crucial role of Will Kidder. Ralph Waite was suggested; Pete knew his work as an actor and was enthusiastic about using him. Fortunately, Ralph was just as enthusiastic about doing the play, and when I listened to him at the first rehearsal I knew we had made a very wise choice. *Laura Dennis*, directed by Jim Houghton, closed the season.

Will Kidder, Lily Dale Kidder, and Pete Davenport, the leading characters in *The Young Man from Atlanta*, all appear in earlier plays of mine: Lily Dale and Pete in *Roots in a Parched Ground*, *Lily Dale*, and *Cousins*, Will Kidder in *Lily Dale* and *Cousins*. We first meet Lily Dale when she is ten and follow her through different phases of her life until we see her at sixty in *The Young Man from Atlanta*. When we first meet Will in *Lily Dale*, he is in his early twenties; he's approaching middle age in *Cousins*; and he's sixty-four in *The Young Man from Atlanta*. Pete Davenport, Lily Dale's stepfather, is in his early thirties when we first meet him and seventy-two in *The Young Man from Atlanta*.

*Roots in a Parched Ground*, *Lily Dale*, and *Cousins* are all part of a nine-play cycle called *The Orphan's Home*. When I finished *Cousins* in the late 1970s, I thought I was through with Will, Lily Dale, and Pete forever; but four years ago I began thinking about the three of them again, cut off from their beginning roots, trying to make a life in the ever-growing Houston; and soon after I began working on my play.

The Will Kidders of this world I've known all my life, North and South—optimistic, hardworking, confident that their world is the best of all possible worlds, admiring business success above all other things. It seemed for many years that Will's private and public world would continue forever on its upward spiral. But it doesn't—and that's the dilemma we find him in at the beginning of the play.

From the very first I've had ambivalent feelings about the character of Lily Dale. In the earlier plays, even as a child, she seemed to me vain and selfish and not very admirable, but when I came to her again in this play I wanted to make her more complex, give her more humanity and vulnerability, always keeping in mind her many faults. Carlin Glynn fortunately loved exploring all these many facets and did much to make her understood by an audience.

Indeed, all the actors—Devon Abner, Christina Burz, Seth Jones, James Pritchett, Frances Foster, Michael Lewis, and Beatrice Winde in addition to Carlin Glynn and Ralph Waite—did much to give the play a compelling life.

The eponymous "young man from Atlanta" never appears. A number of characters in the play have to decide whether the story he has told is the truth or not. Lily Dale wants to believe it. Will does not. It was always interesting to me how different members of the audience came to quite differing conclusions about his truthfulness.

At a benefit for the theatre just before rehearsals began, a letter from Edward Albee to me was read. It said:

# INTRODUCTION

Dear Horton:

Welcome to the club! You will most probably have a frightening experience with the Signature Theatre Company this coming season.

You will discover that you are working with eager, dedicated, talented, resourceful, gentle and thoughtful people whose main concern will be making you happy. This will be frightening.

Even more, they will succeed in making you happy. This will be even more frightening.

Don't fret about it; just go with it.

Have a wonderful season.

Regards,
Edward Albee

He was a true prophet. It was a wonderful season and they did much to make me happy, and I'll always be grateful.

—Horton Foote
May 1995

*The Young Man from Atlanta* was first produced by the Signature Theatre Company in New York City (James Houghton, founding artistic director; Thomas C. Proehl, managing director; Elliot Fox, associate director), and opened on January 27, 1995, with the following cast:

| | |
|---|---|
| Will Kidder | Ralph Waite |
| Tom Jackson | Devon Abner |
| Miss Lacey | Christina Burz |
| Ted Cleveland Jr. | Seth Jones |
| Lily Dale Kidder | Carlin Glynn |
| Pete Davenport | James Pritchett |
| Clara | Frances Foster |
| Carson | Michael Lewis |
| Etta Doris | Beatrice Winde |

It was directed by Peter Masterson. The sets were designed by E. David Cosier; the costumes, by Teresa Snider-Stein and Jonathan Green; the lighting, by Jeffrey S. Koger. The production stage manager was Dean Gray; the assistant stage manager, Casey A. Rafter. Casting was by Jerry Beaver.

# CHARACTERS

Will Kidder
Tom Jackson
Miss Lacey
Ted Cleveland Jr.
Lily Dale Kidder
Pete Davenport
Clara
Carson
Etta Doris

Place: Houston, Texas

Time: Spring, 1950

# ❧ SCENE I ❧

*The lights are brought up on the office at the Sunshine Southern Wholesale Grocery. It is a fairly large, comfortable office.*

*WILL KIDDER, sixty-four, a hearty, burly man with lots of vitality who has worked for this same firm since his early twenties, is at his desk, a telephone nearby, looking at a set of house plans. TOM JACKSON, thirty-five, a colleague and close friend, comes in.*

**TOM:**
Good morning, Will.

**WILL:**
Good morning, Tom.
            *(Indicating the house plans.)*
I was about to put these away now that we've moved into the house. It's a beauty if I do say so myself. Of course, it cost me a fortune, you know. But shoot, I think it's worth every penny.

**TOM:**
What did it end up costing?

**WILL:**
I haven't gotten to—gather all the final figures. But I'd guess well over two hundred thousand. But it's worth it. There is no finer house in Houston. We have the best of everything.
*(A pause.)*
Excuse me, fellow. I got a little short of breath there for a moment.

**TOM:**
You all right, Will?

**WILL:**
Couldn't be better. I just think I overdid a little this week. I was determined to get everything in place.
*(A pause.)*
Truth is, I have a slight heart condition. Nothing serious, the doctor said. I just have to use common sense and not overdo, the doctor said.

**TOM:**
When did you find this out?

**WILL:**
Yesterday. I wanted to get more life insurance, so I had to go to a doctor for a physical, and when the insurance company read his report, they said it was nothing serious, but I'd have to come back in six months for another examination before they could issue the extra insurance.

**TOM:**
Do you have a good doctor?

**WILL:**
Shoot. The best doctor in Houston. Son, I only go to the best. I learned that lesson a long time ago. You get what you pay for.

**TOM:**
I'm sure that's right.
*(He looks at the house plans.)*
It's none of my business, Will, but I was saying to my wife last night, why in this world does he want a big house like that now that there is only two of you?

**WILL:**
Because I want the best. The biggest and the best. I always have. Since I was a boy. We were dirt poor after my father died, and I said to myself then, I'm not going to live like this the rest of my life. Will Kidder, I said, you are going from now on to always have the best. And I have. I live in the best country in the world. I live in the best city. I have the finest wife a man could have, work for the best wholesale produce company in the—

**TOM:**
Was.

**WILL:**
Will be again. I have worked here almost forty years, son. I know its strengths. All of them. We have the best products in the city of Houston, and those we don't have we just have to aggressively compete for. I'm a competitor, son. A born competitor. Nothing fires me up like competition.
*(A pause.)*
My brother, may his soul rest in peace, wasn't. He didn't have a competitive bone in his body. All he ever thought

about was where his next drink of whiskey was coming from. I said to my son, Bill, stay away from whiskey. Whiskey will ruin your life. Bill, I'm happy to say, took my advice.

*(He takes a picture of a young man in his late twenties off his desk.)*

This is my son.

*(TOM takes the photograph and looks at it.)*

My wife had this made for me yesterday.

**TOM:**
A fine-lookin' fellow.

**WILL** *(taking the photograph back):*
Yes. Never met him, did you?

**TOM:**
No.

**WILL** *(indicating signed letters):*
Here, you take care of this.

*(TOM takes them.)*

It doesn't seem possible he's not here any longer. He was a fine young man. One of the best. We weren't anything at all alike, you know.

**TOM:**
No?

**WILL:**
No, nothing. I'm crazy about sports. He never cared for them. Not that he was artistic like his mother. He wasn't. He had a fine math mind. He was a whiz at math. And he loved school. He was never happier than when he was studying. I thought he was going to stay in college forever.

Cost me a fortune. And then the war came along. He was twenty-nine and he volunteered first thing. Couldn't wait to be drafted. Volunteered for the Air Force. He was a bombardier. Came home without a scratch. Made I don't know how many bombing raids and didn't even get a scratch. I thought, my boy has a charmed life for sure. When the war was over I wanted to bring him here in the business, but he would have none of it. He got a job in Atlanta. Why Atlanta, I said. You were born and raised in Houston, Texas, the finest city in the whole of the world. I never could figure out exactly what his job was. I don't think he used any of his math skills as far as I could tell. He traveled a lot. He was on a trip for his company that day. . . .

*(A pause.)*

I still can't believe it.

**TOM:**

Don't go over all that now if it upsets you.

**WILL:**

No. It does me good to talk about it. I can't talk to my wife about it.

*(A pause.)*

He was in Florida for his company and he stopped at this lake to go for a swim. He couldn't swim. Never learned, and I never remember hearing of him going swimming before. Anyway, that's what he did this day. The man that owned the lake was there alone and he said it never occurred to him to ask him if he could swim. He said he went into the bathhouse and changed his clothes and came out and waved to him as he walked into the lake. He said he just kept walking until he was out of sight. The man got concerned when he couldn't see him any longer and he yelled to him and when he got no answer he got his boat and rowed out to where he had last seen him and found his body. He had drowned. He was thirty-seven—thirty-seven. Drowned. Our only child. I wanted to have more, but my wife had such a difficult time when he was born that we never had any more.

**TOM:**

I wonder why, if he couldn't swim?

**WILL:**

That's what everyone asked. It was the middle of the day. Why in the middle of the day in a lake in Florida out in deep, deep water if you can't swim.
*(A pause.)*
Everyone has their theories, and I appreciate their theories, but I'm a realist. I don't need theories. I know what happened. He committed suicide. Why, I don't know.

**TOM:**

Oh, that's terrible.

**WILL:**

I know. I know. I've never told anybody that before. But that's what I think. I always have. I feel close to you, son. I suppose I shouldn't be saying these things even to you. But I have no one else I feel I can confide in.

**TOM:**

Did he leave children?

**WILL:**

No. He never married. If he even went with a girl we never knew about it. I've never told my wife what I thought happened. We never discuss that part of it. We talk about how much we miss him and what a fine man he was and

what a considerate son, and he was certainly that. A fine
and considerate son. My wife has become extremely religious since his death. She was always interested in religion,
but now that's all she thinks about. God this and God that.

**TOM:**
Was your son religious?

**WILL:**
No more than I am. I can take it or leave it. He joined the
Episcopal Church as a young man. Your job was the one
I hoped would interest him here in the company, but it
didn't.
   (MISS LACEY *comes in. She is* WILL'S *secretary.*)

**MISS LACEY:**
Excuse me, Mr. Kidder. There is a call for you.

**WILL:**
Who is it from?

**MISS LACEY:**
That same young man.

**WILL:**
Tell him I'm not here.

**MISS LACEY:**
He'll want to know when you'll be here. He always does.

**WILL:**
Say you don't know.

**MISS LACEY:**
Yes sir.

*(She goes.)*

**WILL:**
That young man was my son's roommate in Atlanta. He was ten years younger than my son. He came here for the funeral and stayed at our house in Bill's old room. He told my wife that our son had become very religious in the year before his death and that every morning you could hear him praying all over their rooming house. I didn't believe it then and I don't believe it now. Sam Curtis, my oldest friend, came to me and said he thought he was a phony and he was making the whole thing up to get money out of us. I said, then get rid of him. Get him out of the house. And he did. Right after the funeral. During the funeral he got hysterical and cried more than my wife. She was comforting him and he was comforting her. He calls once a week to talk to me. God knows what he wants. Money, I suppose. Although he tells my secretary he just wants to stay in touch with Bill's dad. Anyway, that's why I'm glad we're leaving the old house where Bill was raised and going into this brand new house. Even though it's taking all my cash. . . .

*(A pause.)*

Yes, my wife has gotten very religious. She reads the Bible constantly. She was always interested in music, composing and playing the piano, until this happened, and now, she won't go near her music or the piano.

*(MISS LACEY comes back in.)*

**MISS LACEY:**
The young man left his telephone number and asked if you would call him at your convenience.

*(She gives WILL the number on a slip of paper. She*

*goes. He rolls the paper up and throws it in the wastebasket.)*

**WILL:**

He's nervy. I'll say that. He wrote my wife after he left, but I found one of the letters, all about Bill and God, and I told her not to answer. Maybe next time he calls I'll tell him just to keep the hell away from us.

**TOM:**

Maybe you should tell him now.

**WILL:**

No. I'll wait until he calls again. Maybe he'll at last get the message and not call again.

*(A pause. He reaches into the wastebasket and gets the paper with the phone number out and looks at it.)*

My God. This isn't an Atlanta number. This is a Houston number—Lehigh—6-6000—Lehigh 6-6000. That's the downtown YMCA. I work out there. My God. I'd better tell him to stay away.

*(He dials the number.)*

Yes. Randy Carter. . . . R-A-N-D-Y—Randy—Carter.

*(To Tom:)*

I think his name is Randolph, but he always says "I'm Randy Carter." *(To phone)* Yes? . . . Oh. . . . No. No message.

*(He hangs up the phone.)*

He's not there.

*(A pause.)*

My wife's stepfather is living with us. His wife, my wife's mother, has been dead a number of years and he's all alone. His people are all back in Atlanta, Georgia. What's left of them. He moved to Houston when he was a young man of twenty. He married my wife's mother when my wife was only ten, so he is the only father she's ever known. Pete, that's his name. Pete Davenport. I said, Pete, you wouldn't be kin to this roommate of Bill's back in Atlanta? No, he said, all my close relatives that I know of are dead. Well, I said, maybe he's not such a close one. One that you've never heard of. No, he said, I don't think so. I don't think he looks like anyone I knew or was kin to me in Atlanta, Georgia.

*(A pause.)*

I don't know why I'm telling you all this. I don't have anyone else I can confide in, and I feel like you're my son in many ways.

**TOM:**

Thank you. I appreciate that.

**WILL:**

Of course you'll never mention any of this to anyone else in the company.

**TOM:**

Oh, no. I won't say a word. You can trust me.

**WILL:**

I know I can. How's your wife and children?

**TOM:**

Fine. Just fine.

**WILL:**

Lovely family you have, son. Be glad you have more than one child. It is very, very difficult when you lose your only child.

**TOM:**
I know that it must be.

**WILL:**
My wife's brother lost his second son in an air raid over Germany, and of course they grieved, but then they have two more sons to think about and help them carry on. Well—I hope this new house will help us get away from a lot of memories. To celebrate the new house I'm buying my wife a new car.

**TOM:**
Will, we lost three more accounts today. Three of our largest. Carnation Milk is one, and I understand it has been with us since the beginning of the company.

**WILL:**
When did you find this out?

**TOM:**
I just heard it.

**WILL:**
Who told you?

**TOM:**
Mr. Cleveland Jr. He's in his office today.

**WILL:**
Why in the hell didn't he tell me?

**TOM:**
I don't know, sir. Please don't say I told you.

**WILL:**
No.

**TOM:**
I'm sure he'll tell you.

**WILL:**
I'm sure. Well, it doesn't worry me at all.

**TOM:**
Come on, Will.

**WILL:**
We went through the Depression with flying colors, when the rest of Houston was on its knees. Begging for mercy—not us. Not us. We were prospering.
*(TED CLEVELAND JR., forty-four, enters.)*

**TED:**
Hello, Will.

**WILL:**
Hello, Ted. I was just telling Tom how we weathered the Depression with flying colors. Your dad used to say to me, nothing ever gets you down, does it? No, sir. Nothing. Not Roosevelt. Not the New Deal. Not bureaucrats, nothing. I remember the time, Ted, I told your dad I had decided to vote the Republican ticket for the first time, and that if he didn't want to see this country ruined, he'd better do the same. I can't do that, Will, he said, my granddaddy was a captain in the Confederate Army, my mama heads the UDC here in Houston. Hell, I said. What was that war all about? State rights—and who is for state rights? The Republicans or the Democrats? Of course, he couldn't argue with that. So a day later he called me into his office

and said, you've converted me. I'm voting Republican. And he did. Your father was a hell of a man, Ted. They don't make them like that anymore.

**TED:**
No, they sure don't.
>                    *(A pause.)*
Will you excuse us, Tom?

**TOM:**
Sure.
>          *(He puts the letters on WILL'S desk.)*

**WILL:**
No, you look into this.
>          *(TOM takes the letters and leaves.)*

**TED:**
How is your wife, Will?

**WILL:**
Pretty fair. Considering everything.

**TED:**
Terrible about your son. I suppose she's gradually getting over it. Of course, I don't suppose you ever really get over such things. Not a son. Not an only son.

**WILL:**
It's not easy. How are your wife and children?

**TED:**
They're all well, thank you. Spend too much money, but otherwise I can't complain. How do you like Tom?

**WILL:**

He's a fine young man.


**TED:**

I think so.


**WILL:**

I hired him, you know. I trained him.


**TED:**

Yes, I'm aware of that.

*(A pause.)*

The company is going through a bad patch, Will. We've just lost three more accounts. Including Carnation.


**WILL:**

You don't say. When did you hear this?


**TED:**

Yesterday.


**WILL:**

I wish you would have told me this right away. You know I've handled the Carnation account from its beginning with the company. They respect me over there. We've done business together now for over thirty years. And if I do say so myself—


**TED:**

May I be frank, Will?


**WILL:**

Yes sir.

**TED:**
You're the reason they're giving for leaving us.

**WILL:**
Me?

**TED:**
Yes. You. They feel you're not with it any longer, as they say.

**WILL:**
Who says? Not Cochran Judd—why, he and I—

**TED:**
No, not Cochran Judd. He's been fired.

**WILL:**
My God. When?

**TED:**
As of yesterday. There have been a lot of replacements there, I believe. It's a new age, Will. My father wouldn't recognize business as it's done today. Very competitive.

**WILL:**
Shoot. That doesn't scare me. I thrive on competition, Ted. When I started with this company, when your dad and I were young men, that's what made us the success we became. Our competitive spirit. Your dad said to me one day, Will, I've always thought of myself as a competitive man, but you're the most competitive man I've ever known or seen. The most. That is what he said. And he called me into his office just before he died and he said, Will, I'm going to die soon, I know, but I'm going with

peace of mind knowing you are here to help my son run the company. The company we built together, Will.

*(A pause.)*

**TED:**
It's a different ball game, Will. What worked forty years ago, or twenty, or ten, doesn't work anymore. I'm going to have to replace you, Will. You'll have three months' notice beginning today.

**WILL:**
Ted . . .

**TED:**
My hands are tied, Will. We have to change our ways of doing business or we'll go under. We're not competing any longer, Will.

**WILL:**
What kind of changes are you talking about? I can change. . . .

**TED:**
I don't think so, Will. We need younger men in charge here.

**WILL:**
Younger men?

**TED:**
Yes. In their twenties, thirties . . .

**WILL:**
Younger men?

**TED:**
Yes, I'm sorry.
*(He sees the house plans. He points to them.)*
What are these?

**WILL:**
This is the house I built.

**TED:**
Oh, yes. I rode by there the other night to take a look at it. Very handsome.

**WILL:**
Thank you.
*(TED sees BILL's picture.)*

**TED:**
And this is your son?

**WILL:**
Yes.

**TED:**
Very tragic. I know it was quite a blow.

**WILL:**
Yes sir. It was.
*(TED gets up.)*

**TED:**
Well, thank you for being so understanding. I'm sure you know how much I appreciate all you have done for the company through the years.

**WILL:**
Thank you.

*(TED starts out of the room.)*

Ted.

**TED:**
Yes?

**WILL:**
I always thought about going out on my own, but I would never do it, out of loyalty to your father, but now I may be starting my own company.

**TED:**
Oh. Well, I wish you luck. You certainly know what you'll be facing. Do you have enough capital to get going?

**WILL:**
I'll start in a very small way.

**TED:**
Well, good luck to you, Will.

**WILL:**
Thanks.

**TED:**
I suppose under these circumstances you'll be leaving the company right away.

**WILL:**
Yes sir.

**TED:**
Good luck to you again.
> (*TED goes. WILL goes to the phone.*)

**WILL** (*at phone*):
Dawson Motor Company? This is Will Kidder. I'm going to have to cancel the order on the car.
> (*A pause.*)

I understand, and I'm sorry. I am hoping I can have my deposit back. Under the circumstances. . . . I see. I understand. . . . No. I understand.
> (*He hangs up the phone, then picks it up again.*)

Miss Lacey. Ask Tom to come in. Thank you.
> (*He opens the drawer of his desk and begins to go through it, discarding items in the wastebasket.*
> *TOM comes in.*)

Sit down, son. My life is just about to change. And being an optimist, I think for the better. I'm going to try and start my own company. In a modest way for now.

**TOM:**
Oh.

**WILL:**
It's something I've wanted to do for a long time, but I wouldn't out of loyalty to this company, but now. . . .
> (*A pause.*)

I've been fired. Replaced by a younger man.

**TOM:**
I'm sorry.

**WILL:**
I won't lie to you. It's quite a blow to my pride. But never mind. I've had worse blows than this and on I'll go. I'll be

honest with you. It's come at a bad time. I've put a lot of my cash in the new house.

**TOM:**

But you've savings, I'm sure. . . .

**WILL:**

Not much. My savings went into the house. But I have friends in every bank in Houston. I know they'll help me get started. They'll stand by me until I'm on my feet once again. I'm going slow, you know, all I need is a hundred thousand, two hundred thousand. . . .

*(A pause.)*

I hope after I've gotten started that you'll join me. I wouldn't ask you to come aboard just now, because I know you have responsibilities, a wife and children, but once I get going I'm coming back to you and I hope—

*(A pause.)*

Do you know who they've hired to take my place?

**TOM:**

Yes, I do.

**WILL:**

Who is it? Anyone I know?

**TOM:**

Yes. It's me, Will.

*(A pause.)*

I feel terrible about it, but Ted explained that no matter what I did. . . .

**WILL:**

I understand, son. Well, good luck to you.

**TOM:**
Thank you.

**WILL:**
Excuse me, now. I have to make a phone call about my financing.

**TOM:**
Sure.
> (*TOM goes. WILL picks up the phone and dials.*)

**WILL:**
Hello. . . . Yes sir. This is Will Kidder. Will Kidder. I want to come in and talk to you about a proposition that I think you'll find very interesting. . . . Will Kidder. K-I-D-D-E-R. . . . Yes. Kidder.
> (*He continues talking as the lights fade.*)

# ❧ SCENE II ❧

*The lights are brought up on a section of the den in the new house of the WILL KIDDERS. It is a day later; evening.*

*WILL is alone, sitting on the couch. As lights rise, CLARA enters with coffee service, followed by LILY DALE, sixty, and her stepfather, PETE DAVENPORT, seventy-two.*

**LILY DALE:**
Thank you, Clara.

**CLARA:**
You're welcome.
> *(She exits.)*

**LILY DALE:**
It was a lovely supper, wasn't it? I tell you, I believe Clara is the best cook we've ever had. During the war, you

know, Mrs. Roosevelt got all the maids in Houston to join the Disappointment Club.

**PETE:**
Did she? I never heard about that.

**LILY DALE:**
You didn't? It was just awful. A maid would say they were going to work for you. You would arrange the hours and the salary and she would be so nice and polite; then the day she was supposed to start work, she wouldn't show up, and that meant she was a member of the Disappointment Club, whose purpose was to disappoint white people.

**WILL:**
And you think Mrs. Roosevelt was behind that?

**LILY DALE:**
I know she was. Everybody in Houston knows she was. She just hated the South, you know. She took out all her personal unhappiness on the South.

**WILL:**
Shoot. Somebody sold you a bill of goods, Lily Dale. I never cared much for either of the Roosevelts, as you know, but I don't think Mrs. Roosevelt organized the maids in Houston into anything.

**LILY DALE:**
Well, she did.

**WILL:**
All right. She did.

*(A pause.)*

**LILY DALE:**
Daddy?

**WILL:**
What?

**LILY DALE:**
Why are you so cross?

**WILL:**
I don't mean to be cross. I'm tired, I guess. I'm sorry.

**LILY DALE:**
That's all right, Daddy. I guess you have a right to be tired, as hard as you work. He's been so good to me all my life, Pete. Anything I ever wanted, Will got for me.

**PETE:**
I know that.

**LILY DALE:**
When is my new car going to be here, Daddy?

**WILL:**
That may have to wait a while now, Lily Dale. The house and the furnishings just cost more than I figured. I want to get them all paid for before I take on any more debts.

**LILY DALE:**
The house is so beautiful, Will.
> *(A pause.)*
I wish Bill could have seen it.
> *(A pause.)*
I miss Bill so much, Daddy.

**WILL:**

I know.

**LILY DALE:**

Not that we saw much of him these last years, but it was just knowing you could call him on the phone when you wanted to. Or that he'd be with us at Christmas. The minute he'd come home for Christmas he'd ask me what new pieces I had composed, remember? And then he'd say, play it for me. I'd say, you haven't called your daddy at the office, and he'd say, time enough for that. I want to hear your new pieces right this very minute.

*(A pause.)*

I don't compose anymore, Pete.

**PETE:**

I know.

**LILY DALE:**

I haven't gone near the piano since Bill died. That all seems too frivolous to me now. Vanity. Vanity. Things of this world. Vanity. Vanity.

*(WILL gets up.)*

**WILL:**

I'm tired. I'm going to bed. Glad to have you here with us, Pete.

**PETE:**

Thank you. Nice to be here.

*(WILL starts out of the room, then pauses.)*

**WILL:**

Lily Dale, that roommate Bill had back in Atlanta is here in Houston.

**LILY DALE:**
Oh?

**WILL:**
He called the office today. Has he called here?

**LILY DALE:**
No.

**WILL:**
If he does, let him know we want nothing to do with him.

**LILY DALE:**
You told me that before, Daddy. I still don't understand what happened to turn you so against him. You seemed to like him so much at first. You seem—

**WILL:**
I have my reasons, Lily Dale.

**LILY DALE:**
I'm sure you do.

**WILL:**
Good night.

**LILY DALE:**
Good night.

**PETE:**
Good night.

*(WILL goes.)*

**LILY DALE:**
I don't know why he's turned against him. Do you?

**PETE:**
No.

**LILY DALE:**
What did you think of him, Pete?

**PETE:**
I didn't say more than two words to him, Lily Dale, the whole time he was here.

**LILY DALE:**
I don't care what Daddy says. I think he is a very sweet boy. I can't tell you what it meant to me when he told me how religious Bill had become. Why, he said every morning you could hear him pray all over the boardinghouse. He said they were the most beautiful prayers he had ever heard. He said everybody in the boardinghouse just stopped whatever they were doing to listen to him pray.
*(A pause.)*
Allie Temple committed suicide, I heard today. She took poison.

**PETE:**
She was from Harrison, wasn't she?

**LILY DALE:**
Yes, but she hadn't lived there for years. Her husband, Lawrence, killed himself. I guess it was twenty years ago. He hung himself. Alice was an atheist, you know. I went over to see her a month or so ago and I said, Alice, my son Bill told me the last time he was at home, there are no atheists in foxholes. Is that so, she said, very sarcastically. You aren't really an atheist, are you, Alice? I am, she said, confirmed. My heavens, I told her, I couldn't ever in this world be an atheist. God has been too good to me.

He certainly has been good to you, she said, again most
sarcastically. Only why did this good God let your son
commit suicide? What on earth are you talking about, I
said. His death was an accident. If it was an accident, she
said, what was he doing in a lake over his head, when he
couldn't swim? It was a hot day, I said, that's why he went
for a swim. And how many swims had he ever gone to
before? Ask your God to explain that. And she upset me
so, Pete, that I couldn't stop trembling and my heart
started racing so, I thought I would have a heart attack.
And I just had to call that sweet roommate of his in Atlanta, even though Daddy had told me never to, and I told
him exactly what Alice had told me. He said there was not
a word of truth in it, and he had talked to him from Florida
the night before on the telephone and the whole time they
talked about God. So, I felt very relieved after that, and I
thanked God, got on my knees and thanked God for send-
ing this sweet friend of Bill's to tell me once again of Bill's
faith in God. I could never be an atheist. Could you, Pete?

**PETE:**
No.

**LILY DALE:**
My cousin Willa Thornton is, you know. Least she says
she is. She says all the terrible things that have happened
to her family make her an atheist. Pete, you do believe in
God, don't you?

**PETE:**
Yes, I do.

**LILY DALE:**
I'm glad of that. I wish you'd start going to church with
me, Pete.

**PETE:**
Maybe I will one Sunday.

**LILY DALE:**
Will won't go with me to church. He says he believes in God, but he can't stand church. Don't ever tell Will I called that friend of Bill's. I've never done anything in my life I felt Will disapproved of, but this one time I had to disobey him.

*(A pause.)*

Pete, if I tell you something, promise you won't breathe it to another soul?

**PETE:**
I promise.

**LILY DALE:**
Every time I feel blue over missing Bill, I call his friend and I ask him to tell me again about Bill and his prayers and he does so so sweetly. And I've been helping him too, Pete.

**PETE:**
How have you been helping him?

**LILY DALE:**
Loaning him money. Well, not loaning it to him exactly. Although he says that's how he feels about it. You know, he's been so blue and depressed since Bill died that he couldn't keep his mind on his job and he got fired and so I sent him five thousand dollars until he could get himself together, and then—

**PETE:**
Is that all you sent him, Lily Dale?

**LILY DALE:**
No, not all.

**PETE:**
How much have you given him, Lily Dale?

**LILY DALE:**
I don't know exactly. I've got it written down somewhere. His mother got sick and needed an operation and I sent him ten thousand for her and his sister's husband deserted her and she has three small children and so I sent—

**PETE:**
Lily Dale.

**LILY DALE:**
It's my money, Pete. I prayed about it and God said that's what Bill would want me to do, and Randy, that's the name of Bill's friend, said he was sure it was, because he said Bill was going to make him the beneficiary of his life insurance, and that's another reason he knew he didn't commit suicide, because he hadn't had time to change his life insurance making him the beneficiary.

**PETE:**
Lily Dale.

**LILY DALE:**
It's my money, Pete. Will gave me the money every Christmas and he always said, spend it like you want to, and I never spent any of it because there was nothing I needed or wanted and I kept it all untouched, just in case one day Bill might need something to buy a house when he got married. . . .

*(A pause.)*

Do you know what's troubling Daddy, Pete? He seemed so quiet at supper. So depressed. It's not like Daddy to be depressed.

**PETE:**
No.

**LILY DALE:**
Do you know what's troubling him?

**PETE:**
Yes, I do.

**LILY DALE:**
What is it, Pete?

**PETE:**
I don't think I can tell you.

**LILY DALE:**
Why can't you tell me, Pete?

**PETE:**
Because I think Will would be mad at me if I did.

**LILY DALE:**
Did he ask you not to tell me?

**PETE:**
Yes.

**LILY DALE:**
Do you think he'll ever tell me?

**PETE:**
I think he will. Yes, I do.

**LILY DALE:**
When?

**PETE:**
At the right time.

**LILY DALE:**
You scare me, Pete—is it something bad?

**PETE:**
I can't say any more, Lily Dale.

**LILY DALE:**
I won't sleep tonight now for worry. I've got lots to worry me, Pete.

**PETE:**
I'm sorry.

**LILY DALE:**
I haven't slept hardly a night through since Bill died.

**PETE:**
I'm sure.

**LILY DALE:**
Will just sleeps the whole night through. I know he misses Bill, but it doesn't seem to affect his sleep.
*(A pause.)*
I have another worry now, Pete. I knew Bill's friend was in Houston. He's been out here twice today. He needs a job so badly. I'm praying that Will has a change of heart

and finds a job for him at his company. If he knows how Will feels about him he doesn't let on. He told me he had been calling him. He needs a job and he needs a father, he's hoping Will will be a father to him. He said Bill was like a father to him, gave him advice in all things. He never knew his own father. He died when he was two. I know what that's like, Pete, having lost my own father when I was eight. But I was lucky because Mama married you and you became a wonderful father to me, but, unfortunately, his mother married a man that was a drunkard and he beat him and his sister. I've asked him to visit me here in the afternoons while Will is at work, whenever he gets blue, but you mustn't ever tell Will this, Pete, until God changes his heart, and he will change his heart, that I know, because Will is a good man, a kind man. Don't you think he will change about this, Pete?

**PETE:**
Maybe so. I hope so, if that's what you want.

**LILY DALE:**
It's certainly what I want.
    *(WILL comes in. He is in his robe and pajamas.)*
Couldn't you sleep?

**WILL:**
No.

**LILY DALE:**
I thought you were sleepy.

**WILL:**
I thought so, too. But I'm not.

**LILY DALE:**
Anything worrying you, Will?

**WILL:**
To tell you the truth there is. I was going to wait a day or two before telling you this, but I guess I'd better get it over with.

**PETE:**
You want me to leave, Will?

**WILL:**
No, you stay. You know about it anyway. I've been fired, Lily Dale.

**LILY DALE:**
What?

**WILL:**
Fired.

**LILY DALE:**
From the company?

**WILL:**
Yes.

**LILY DALE:**
Why on earth—

**WILL:**
They are replacing me with a younger man. Tom Jackson.

**LILY DALE:**
Tom Jackson. Why, you hired him, trained him.

**WILL:**

I know. I know. He feels terrible about it.

**LILY DALE:**

Will, if he feels so terrible about it, why—

**WILL:**

There's nothing he can do about it. If he didn't take the job they'd just give it to someone else. They want younger men.

**LILY DALE:**

Who does?

**WILL:**

Ted Cleveland Jr.

**LILY DALE:**

Oh, I think it's scandalous. What will you do, Will?

**WILL:**

I'm going to start my own company if I can get one of the banks to finance me. They told me I could stay on at the company for three months, but I said I wanted to leave right away. I'll spend tomorrow talking to some of my banker friends about a loan.

*(A pause.)*

I hate to ask this, Lily Dale, but I may need some cash. How much do you have left of those Christmas checks I've given you?

**LILY DALE:**

Let's see—

**WILL:**
I'll just need to borrow it back for a month or so.

**LILY DALE:**
Well—and then you have Bill's money that you gave him that you were going to give to me after he died—

**WILL:**
That money was all spent.

**LILY DALE:**
Spent?

**WILL:**
Yes.

**LILY DALE:**
How? Bill never spent money on anything that I knew of. He spent no money on clothes; you gave him his car. He didn't even have an apartment—he lived in a boarding-house.

**WILL:**
That's perfectly true.

**LILY DALE:**
Then how did he spend it, Will?

**WILL:**
I don't know how he spent it. There was nothing in his room.

**LILY DALE:**
I don't understand it.

**WILL:**
Neither do I. But that's how it is. His life insurance barely
paid the funeral expenses. Would you mind going down
in the morning and getting your money? I gave you five
thousand for fifteen Christmases, so you should have at
least seventy-five thousand unless you've spent some of
it.

*(A pause.)*

Have you spent any of it?

**LILY DALE:**
Not that I remember.

**WILL:**
Thank God. I'm going to need every nickel I can get until
I get this all straightened out, and don't look so upset,
honey. I will get it straightened out. We'll be back on our
feet before you can turn around good. You know your
husband. I always land on my feet.

*(A pause.)*

Well, I feel better now that's off my chest. I think I can
sleep now. Are you coming to bed, honey?

**LILY DALE:**
I'll be along later.

*(WILL goes. There is a pause. LILY DALE goes to the
door to listen to see if he has really gone to his room.
When she thinks he has, she turns to PETE.)*

Pete, what am I going to do? Over half that money is
gone.

**PETE:**
My God, Lily Dale.

**LILY DALE:**
I don't think there is twenty-five thousand left.

**PETE:**
My God.

**LILY DALE:**
Pete, could you loan me some money?

**PETE:**
All I have, Lily Dale, is the money that's left from the sale of your mama and my duplex.

**LILY DALE:**
How much is left, Pete?

**PETE:**
Thirty-five thousand.

**LILY DALE:**
Will you give that to me, please, Pete?

**PETE:**
Lily Dale, it's all I have in this world except for my social security. If I should get sick . . .

**LILY DALE:**
I'll find a way to pay you back, Pete—as soon as Will gets on his feet again, he'll give me back the money I've loaned him and I'll give it to you right away.
                    *(A pause.)*
Please, Pete.

**PETE:**
Lily Dale—

**LILY DALE:**
Please, Pete. Please—

**PETE:**
All right. I'll get it in the morning.

**LILY DALE:**
Oh, thank you, Pete. Thank you. You've been so good to me all my life and I'm so grateful to you, Pete. I am. I am.

**PETE:**
I know. I know, Lily Dale.
*(WILL comes back in.)*

**LILY DALE:**
Still not sleepy, Will?

**WILL:**
No.

**LILY DALE:**
Would you like me to fix you some hot milk? That might make you sleepy.

**WILL:**
No, thank you.
*(A pause.)*
I might as well come out with it. I'm going to have to ask you to help me, Pete.

**PETE:**
I want to help in any way I can, Will. You know that. I think for one thing I should start paying board and room as long as I stay here.

**WILL:**
Come on, Pete.

**PETE:**
I think I should. I wanted to from the beginning but Lily Dale said you would never hear of it.

**WILL:**
That's right, and I still won't hear of it. You really hurt me, Pete, even mentioning it.

**PETE:**
I meant no offense, Will.
> *(A pause.)*
In what way can I help you, Will?

**WILL:**
How much do you have in savings?

**PETE:**
Well, let's see. Thirty-five thousand dollars, more or less.

**WILL:**
Thirty-five thousand?

**PETE:**
Uh-huh—more or less. That's what I got when I sold the duplex. I have it in savings in case I get sick or—when I die, of course, if it's all still there, I was going to leave it to you and Lily Dale.
> *(A pause.)*
Why did you want to know about my savings, Will?

**WILL:**
Pete—

**LILY DALE:**
You want me to go, Will?

**WILL:**
No, you stay here. You might as well hear it too. I think you know I want to start my own business in a very conservative way. I went to a few banks yesterday to test the waters and it's clear they are not going to loan me all the money I need. Now, I think you know me well enough that I don't have to tell you that I am a very responsible man.

**PETE:**
You're certainly that, Will.

**WILL:**
I'm competitive, a hard worker—

**PETE:**
All of that, Will.

**WILL:**
But right now I've got my back against the wall. I need conservatively to start my own business three hundred thousand dollars, but I feel sure now the banks won't help out unless I have some money of my own. Now, Lily Dale is going to loan me her seventy-five thousand dollars.

**LILY DALE:**
Now, I'm not sure it's seventy-five thousand dollars, Daddy.

**WILL:**
All right. More or less. And Pete, if you could loan me just for a month or so your thirty-five thousand—that would

give me a hundred and ten thousand, and I could put up
the house as security, and—

**PETE:**
Well—

**WILL:**
I'd pay you good interest, Pete. I'd give you a note and
better interest than you could get anywhere in Houston.
I'll pay you back out every first-earned dollar and I'd give
you an interest in the business besides.
>                    *(LILY DALE begins to cry.)*
What's the matter, Lily Dale?
>                    *(She continues crying.)*
What's the matter?

**LILY DALE:**
You tell him, Pete. I can't bear to tell him.

**PETE:**
Lily Dale, I don't want to get mixed up in this. You better
tell him.

**LILY DALE:**
I can't, Pete. I can't. . . .

**PETE:**
All right.
>                    *(A pause.)*
Lily Dale asked me to loan her my thirty-five thousand so
you wouldn't find out.
>                    *(A pause.)*

**WILL:**
Find out what?

**PETE:**
You're sure you want me to tell him, Lily Dale?

**LILY DALE:**
Yes. He has to know.

**PETE:**
Well, Lily Dale has given part of the money you gave her—

**WILL:**
Part? How much?

**PETE:**
I don't know how much. How much, Lily Dale?

**LILY DALE:**
Thirty-five thousand dollars. I believe.

**WILL:**
You believe?

**LILY DALE:**
Yes, I believe.

**WILL:**
Who did you give it to?
                    *(A pause.)*
Was it a loan?

**LILY DALE:**
They say they consider it so, but I didn't give it as a loan.

**WILL:**
I don't understand.

**LILY DALE:**
It was given as a gift. I didn't ask to be paid back.

**WILL:**
Can they pay you back?

**LILY DALE:**
I don't think so. Not right away, anyway.
*(A pause.)*
You told me, Will, the money was mine to do what I wanted to with it. I had saved it thinking I'll give it to Bill when he married to buy a house, but then he died.

**WILL:**
Who did you give it to?
*(A pause.)*
Do you know who she gave it to, Pete?

**PETE:**
Yes.

**WILL:**
Who?

**PETE:**
I'd rather Lily Dale would tell you.
*(LILY DALE is crying.)*

**WILL:**
Will you please stop crying, Lily Dale, and tell me who you gave the money to?
*(A pause.)*
Lily Dale—

**LILY DALE:**
That sweet young friend of Bill's.

**WILL:**
Oh, my God. I told you not to go near him. Ever again.

**LILY DALE:**
I know you did.

**WILL:**
What the hell do you mean giving him my money?

**LILY DALE:**
You said it was my money. You said when you gave it to me I could do with it like I wanted to.

**WILL:**
Not to throw it away on bums, I didn't.

**LILY DALE:**
I don't think he's a bum, Will.

**WILL:**
Well, I do. B-U-M—bum. Get it back from him. He's at the YMCA. Call him up and get it back. Tell him if he doesn't give it back I'll have him arrested. I'm going down there right now and get it from him. I'll break his neck. You lied to me, Lily Dale. Goddamn it. You told me you hadn't been near that boy. You lied to me. Goddamn it. Why did you lie to me? Why? Why? Why?
*(A pause.)*

**LILY DALE:**
I don't know. I felt sorry for him. He lost his job because he was so upset over Bill's death, and then his mother

46

got sick and needed a serious operation, and then his sister had three small children and her husband deserted her.

**WILL:**
Bull.

**LILY DALE:**
That's the truth. That's what he told me.

**WILL:**
Bull. You've been taken for a fool, woman. All right. I'm going to sell this goddamn house and use the money in my business. We'll live in a tourist court. I'm firing Clara tomorrow. You can do the housework for a change. I'm sick of working myself to death for you to give my good money to deadbeats.
*(WILL goes.)*

**LILY DALE:**
Oh, Pete. Go to him. He's all upset. Calm him down. Go to him, Pete.

**PETE:**
Maybe you should go to him, Lily Dale.

**LILY DALE:**
No, he doesn't want to see me. He hates me now. Go to him, Pete. Please.
*(PETE goes. LILY DALE puts her head in her hands. She is trying to control her crying. PETE comes back in.)*

**PETE:**
Call his doctor, Lily Dale. He thinks it's his heart.

**LILY DALE:**
My God, my God.
> *(She goes to the phone as the lights fade.)*

# ❦ SCENE III ❦

*The lights are brought up on the study. It is a week later. CLARA, the maid, is there dusting. LILY DALE enters.*

**LILY DALE:**
Oh, hello, Clara.

**CLARA:**
That young man from Atlanta says he was a friend of your son's came by again this morning looking for you.

**LILY DALE:**
What did you tell him?

**CLARA:**
I told him you weren't home. He called twice before he came over.

**LILY DALE:**

Oh, Clara. I'm a nervous wreck. Everything is just so awful.

**CLARA:**

Where is your Christian faith?

**LILY DALE:**

I know. I know. Thank you for reminding me. And I need all the Christian faith I can muster. Clara, let me tell you, I haven't slept for five nights. I am a nervous wreck. I have been deceived, I have been so deceived it has just broken my heart.

**CLARA:**

Who deceived you, darling?

**LILY DALE:**

That young man. Bill's friend from Atlanta.

**CLARA:**

How did he deceive you, darling?

**LILY DALE:**

In all ways. You see, I had some money that Will gave me over a number of Christmases, and after Bill died this young man came for the funeral and he told me Bill had become very religious and that they were devoted to each other and that Bill was going to make him the beneficiary in his will and he. . . .

*(She begins to cry.)*

**CLARA:**
Now, now.

**LILY DALE:**
I feel so betrayed, so hurt, so humiliated. Dear God, why?
Why?
*(A pause.)*
Anyway, he said he was so upset over Bill's death he
couldn't work, and I sent him money to help out until he
could find work, and then he said he had a sick mother
who needed an operation and a sister—
*(She cries again.)*
Oh, it's just awful, Clara. It's just awful.

**CLARA:**
Now, now.

**LILY DALE:**
And I gave him money, and then Will lost his job and said
he needed to borrow that money he had given me and I
went to my stepfather to ask him to loan me money to
make up for the money I had given Bill's friend and before
my stepfather could get me the money Will asked if he
could borrow the money from my stepfather so I had to
tell him what I'd done with my money, and he was furious
of course and he had his heart attack and he almost died.

**CLARA:**
Well, he didn't die now. So you can thank God for that.

**LILY DALE:**
I know. I know, and I am thankful for that. But it isn't bad
enough I deceived Will and gave the money without telling
him, although it was my money to do with like I wanted,
he always said.

**CLARA:**
Well, then.

**LILY DALE:**
But then yesterday a distant relative of Pete's from Atlanta showed up here named Carson and Pete asked Carson if he had known Bill and his friend in Atlanta and he said he had, and he said that Bill was a fine fellow, but he didn't care much for his friend, who he had known all his life. And Pete asked him how Bill's friend's sick mother was and he said he had no mother living, that he had no family at all since he was an only child, and Pete asked him about Bill being religious and he said it was the first he had heard of it, that he had a room in the boarding-house, too, and that if he ever prayed it was to himself and he hadn't heard a single prayer from Bill the whole time he lived there. Oh, Clara.

**CLARA:**
Now, now.

**LILY DALE:**
Will is not half speaking to me now. I don't know what's going to become of us, Clara. Pete tells me we are in very bad shape financially. Will can't work now even if he wanted to, and we have no money except what I have left from my Christmas gifts.

**CLARA:**
God is going to take care of you.

**LILY DALE:**
You think so?

**CLARA:**
He takes care of me. I have lots to worry me, too, you know. Some mornings I just feel like not getting out of bed, but I say, Clara, get on up. God is gonna take care

of you, and just look around you, you've got this beautiful brand-new house.

**LILY DALE:**
Which is paid for. Thank God. But Pete tells me the furniture is not. I said, Daddy, I don't need new furniture, let's make do with the furniture we have in our old house. No, he said, I want everything new here.
(*PETE comes in with his relative CARSON.*)

**PETE:**
Lily Dale, this is my great-nephew, Carson.

**LILY DALE:**
Hello, Carson. Welcome to Houston.

**CARSON:**
Thank you.

**PETE:**
Carson brought along a picture of my sister, who was his grandmother. I wouldn't have recognized her. She married a Mr. Stewart. She had four children, including Carson's mother.

**LILY DALE:**
Oh? Sit down, Carson.

**PETE:**
Carson says they're all dead except his older sister Vivian and his youngest sister, Susette.

**CARSON:**
Vivian never married. Susette married and has six chil-

dren. Two of them not quite right. It's a real burden for her.

**LILY DALE:**
My goodness. This is Clara, Carson. She works here for us.

**CLARA:**
How do you do.

**CARSON:**
How do you do.

**CLARA:**
I have a sister who has a child that has fits. She can't leave the house, because she has to put every living minute watching that child.

**LILY DALE:**
Pete says you knew Bill?

**CARSON:**
Oh, yes. He was a fine fellow.

**LILY DALE:**
He certainly was that.

**CARSON:**
I knew his roommate too. I didn't think too much of him.

**LILY DALE:**
No?

**CARSON:**
No. A big talker.

**LILY DALE:**
I see.

**CARSON:**
Always bragging.

**LILY DALE:**
Where did he work?

**CARSON:**
He never worked as far as I know.
*(WILL comes in. He is in his pajamas and robe.)*

**LILY DALE:**
Do you think you ought to be out of bed, Will?

**WILL:**
If I didn't think so, I wouldn't be.

**PETE:**
Will, this is my great-nephew, Carson.

**WILL:**
Please to know you, Carson.
*(A pause.)*
How do you like Houston?

**CARSON:**
Fine, what little I've seen of it.

**WILL:**
Where are you staying?

**CARSON:**
At the YMCA.

**WILL:**
Oh, yes.

**LILY DALE:**
Clara, did you ever hear of the maids organizing Disappointment Clubs in Houston during the war?

**CLARA:**
No ma'am. I sure didn't.

**LILY DALE:**
Maybe you were right, Will.

**WILL:**
I know I'm right about Mrs. Roosevelt.
*(The front doorbell rings.)*

**CLARA:**
Excuse me.
*(She goes to the door.)*

**CARSON:**
What are Disappointment Clubs?

**LILY DALE:**
Well, I was always told that Mrs. Roosevelt—
*(TOM JACKSON comes in. He has a bouquet of flowers.)*
Well, hello, Tom. Will, Tom is here.

**WILL:**
Hello, Tom.

**TOM:**
Hello, young man. I thought I'd find you in bed.

**WILL:**
I just got up. I get tired of the bed, Tom.

**TOM:**
I brought these flowers for you.

**WILL:**
Thank you, Tom.
                    *(He takes them.)*

**LILY DALE:**
Aren't they pretty.
                    *(Calling:)*
Clara!

**WILL:**
This is my stepfather-in-law, Tom. Pete Davenport.

**TOM:**
How do you do.
                    *(They shake hands.)*

**WILL:**
And what's your name, young man?

**CARSON:**
Carson.

**TOM:**
Hello, Carson. Tom Jackson.
                    *(They shake hands.)*

**PETE:**
He's my great-nephew. He's just come here from Atlanta.
He's looking for a job. You don't know of a job, do you?

**TOM:**
Not right offhand.

**WILL:**
Tom works at my old company.

**LILY DALE:**
I don't see how they had the heart to do that to Will, Tom. As hard as he worked for that company through the years.

**WILL:**
Let's change the subject, Lily Dale. Tom had nothing to do with it.

**LILY DALE:**
I know he didn't have anything to do with it, Daddy. Carson, my husband worked for a company for—

**WILL:**
Let's change the subject, Lily Dale. The doctor says I'm not supposed to dwell on all of that. It's not good for me.

**LILY DALE:**
All right, Will, I'm sorry.
     (*CLARA comes in.*)

**CLARA:**
You wanted me.

**LILY DALE:**
Yes. Please take those pretty flowers and put them in water and a vase.
     (*CLARA takes them.*)

**CLARA:**
They are pretty. I called my friend Lucille and I asked her if she ever knew of them Disappointment Clubs. She said she'd heard of them, but wouldn't have anything to do with them.

**LILY DALE:**
See, Will? Ask your friend if Mrs. Roosevelt was behind it all.

**CLARA:**
Yes, ma'am.
> (*She takes the flowers and goes.*)

**WILL:**
I think the banks in Houston are all running Disappointment Clubs. I've been doing business with almost every bank in Houston in one way or another for forty years—when I went to see them yesterday about starting my own business they looked at me like they never heard of me.

**TOM:**
That happens. Then one day you go in and talk to someone else and it'll be a different story.

**WILL:**
Anyway, I can't work for a while.

**TOM:**
When you get stronger I wish you'd come down to the company. I was talking to Ted last night. He thinks he may be able to find something for you to do—less responsibility, I suppose.

**WILL:**

No, Tom. I'll never go back there. I was very hurt by that, you know.

**TOM:**

I know you were, and I don't blame you.

**CARSON:**

Do you still work, Uncle Pete?

**PETE:**

No, son, I retired a long time ago. I was with the Southern Pacific. Engineer.

**CARSON:**

My daddy was an engineer.

**PETE:**

Is that right.

**CARSON:**

He drank, though, and they fired him. Mama says he never left the house—that she didn't pray he wouldn't have a wreck because of his drinking.

*(The front doorbell rings.)*

**PETE:**

You better not drink and run engines. I never drank in my life. I worked since I was fourteen until I retired.

**CARSON:**

Mama says Grandma says you were always a hard worker. When was the last time you were in Atlanta, Uncle Pete?

**PETE:**
Thirty years, I guess.

**CARSON:**
You wouldn't know it now.

**PETE:**
I guess not.

(*CLARA enters.*)

**CLARA:**
That young man is here again.

**WILL:**
What young man?

**CLARA:**
Mr. Bill's roommate from Atlanta.

**LILY DALE:**
Tell him we're not here.

**CLARA:**
He can see you all in here.

**LILY DALE:**
Tell him we're busy.

**WILL:**
Let me tell him.

(*He starts up.*)

**LILY DALE:**
Now, Daddy. You must not get excited. Just keep calm.
Clara, tell him we can't see him and not to come anymore.

**CARSON:**
Is that Bill's old roommate? He's bad news.
(*LILY DALE begins to cry. She starts out of the room.*)

**LILY DALE:**
Excuse me.

(*She goes.*)

**CARSON:**
Did I say something to upset somebody?

**WILL:**
No. Don't worry about it.

**CARSON:**
I was telling Great-Uncle Pete that he is nothing but a four-flusher.

**PETE:**
Let's change the subject, son.

**CARSON:**
Sure. Whatever you say.

**TOM:**
Ted said he'd like to come by and see you, but he wasn't sure you'd want him to.

**WILL:**
I'd just as soon he'd not come.

**TOM:**
He said he sent you a get-well card.

## SCENE III

**WILL:**
I got it.

*(A pause.)*

**TOM:**
Well, I guess I'd better be on my way. I don't want to overtire you. I hope you'll be feeling better soon, Will.

**WILL:**
Thank you.

*(WILL gets up.)*

**TOM:**
Don't get up, Will. I can find my way out. Take care of yourself, Will. Tell Lily Dale goodbye for me, Will.

*(He turns to PETE and CARSON.)*

Nice to have met you both.

**CARSON:**
Same here.

**PETE:**
Nice to have met you, sir.

*(TOM goes.)*

**WILL:**
He was the one took my job. I brought him into the company and trained him and they gave him my job. I didn't think I felt any hard feelings toward him, but I do. God help me. I do. I gave my life for that company, you know.

**PETE:**
Now, Will—

**WILL:**

Of course, I realize now, I've been foolish. I spent too much on this house, I should have saved more. But I'm still comparatively a young man, you know. Sixty-four ain't old.

**CARSON:**

Who's sixty-four?

**PETE:**

Will.

**CARSON:**

How old are you, Great-Uncle Pete?

**PETE:**

None of your business. I don't tell my age.

**CARSON:**

I'm twenty-seven.

**PETE:**

Well, I'm older than you are. I'll tell you that much.

**WILL:**

I gave Bill a hundred thousand dollars at least over the years, and I thought as frugal as he was he was saving every penny of it, investing it. I don't know what he made on his job. I don't think a whole lot—that is why I gave him money every year, so he would have a nest egg, and he squandered it.

**PETE:**

Now, that's water over the dam, Will.

**WILL:**
And Lily Dale giving money behind my back. . . .

**PETE:**
Come on, Will. You're getting all exercised. That's not good for your heart.

*(LILY DALE comes in.)*

**LILY DALE:**
Tom go?

**WILL:**
Yes.

*(CLARA comes in. She has the flowers. She puts them on a table.)*

**LILY DALE:**
Aren't they pretty?

**WILL:**
Take them out of here. I don't want to look at them. Just reminds me of the company.

**CLARA:**
Where shall I put them?

**WILL:**
Take them home with you.

**CLARA:**
Yes sir.

*(She takes the flowers and goes.)*

**WILL:**
When I went to work for that company I was twenty-six.

And we just had Bill and I could hardly get by on the salary I made. Somebody told me about the produce company just starting out and needing someone that was a go-getter and aggressive and I figured that was me. I went up to where the business was then and I met Ted Cleveland Sr. and we hit it off right away and I went to work the next week and the company prospered. And then he died and his son took over.

*(A pause.)*

You want to know something? His son is no business man. He's on the golf course more than in his office. You know what I prophesy? I gave him six months, a year, now I'm not there, and he will lose everything, and that's what sickens me. Forty years of hard work and he will lose everything. Let him get all the twenty-year-olds and thirty-year-olds he wants. They can't prop him up. They can't.

*(A pause.)*

But I was foolish too, you know. I should have seen this coming. I should have saved money. I don't need luxuries or fine cars and fine houses. I'm a simple man at heart. I'm a country boy at heart, and all I want to do is work, and now they tell me I can't work. They've taken my work away from me.

**PETE:**
You'll work again.

**WILL:**
Where?

*(A pause.)*

**LILY DALE:**
Will—

**WILL:**
What?

**LILY DALE:**
The money I had left I put in your account.

**WILL:**
Thank you.

**PETE:**
I have a check for you too, Will.

**WILL:**
I don't want your money now, Pete.

**PETE:**
What about your business?

**WILL:**
When I'm feeling better, I'll think about starting a business, and if I do I'll come to you again at that time.

**PETE:**
Promise me that if you need the money you'll ask me for it.

**WILL:**
I promise.

(*CLARA comes in.*)

**CLARA:**
Miss Lily Dale, that gentleman that was just here says give this to Mr. Will.

**LILY DALE:**

Thank you, Clara.

*(LILY DALE gives WILL the letter and he opens it. He takes out a check.)*

Is that a check, Will?

**WILL:**

Yes. It's for three months' salary.

*(A pause.)*

I wish I could afford to tear it up, but I can't. It's a hell of a thing, isn't it? You work for a company, give them your life blood for forty years, and—

**LILY DALE** *(interrupting)*:

Not forty years, Will. You went there at twenty-six and you're sixty-four. What's twenty-six from sixty-four, Pete?

**CARSON:**

Thirty-eight.

**LILY DALE:**

Thirty-eight.

*(WILL begins to cry.)*

**PETE:**

Come on, Will. Don't give in to your feelings. You're just tired. Now you're gonna feel differently about all this when you've rested.

**WILL** *(wiping his eyes)*:

Thirty-eight years. Where did they go? There was the house on Hawthorne and then the larger house on Kipling. There was— I saw the city growing all around me. There

is no stopping it, I thought, and there is no stopping anyone with vision and competitiveness. . . .
>                    *(A pause.)*

**CARSON:**
How big is Houston?

**PETE:**
God knows—too big, I think now sometimes.

**CARSON:**
I met a fellow at the YMCA that said it was going to be
the largest city in the South, and I said, hold on, mister,
I came from Atlanta and it's going to be the largest city
in the South.

**WILL:**
It is like hell. Houston is the largest city in the South, and
I tell you what, I give it ten years, fifteen, twenty, it will
be the largest city in America, the largest and the richest.
If I were only a young man again . . .
>                    *(A pause.)*
But I'm not a young man. I'm sixty-four years old and I
have been fired and I have to keep reminding myself of
that.

**LILY DALE:**
Will, sixty-four isn't old. I'm sixty and I don't feel old at
all. I don't—
>        *(WILL gives her a look. She shuts up.)*
I guess you don't want to hear my opinion.

**WILL:**
I guess I don't.
>        *(He gets up and slowly leaves the room.)*

**LILY DALE:**
Carson, go see he gets back to his room safely.

**CARSON:**
Yes, ma'am.

**LILY DALE:**
My God, Pete. He's still mad at me. . . .
*(CARSON goes. We hear WILL offstage speaking loudly
to CARSON.)*

**PETE:**
He'll get over it, Lily Dale. Give him time.
*(CARSON comes back in.)*
Did he get to his room all right?

**CARSON:**
I don't know. He told me to stop following him around, he
wasn't a goddamned baby. Do you really think Houston is
going to be the largest city in America?

**PETE:**
I don't know, son.
*(WILL comes back in.)*

**WILL:**
I've got some pride left. I'm not going to take Ted Jr.'s
goddamn check.
*(He hands it to LILY DALE.)*
Here, Lily Dale, give it to your boyfriend from Atlanta.
*(She cries and leaves the room. He tears the check
up. He throws it in the wastebasket as the
lights fade.)*

# ❧ SCENE IV ❧

*The lights are brought up on the study. It's the next day. LILY DALE is sitting on the sofa with her Bible. CLARA enters.*

**CLARA:**
I met someone who used to work for you a long time ago. Etta Doris Meneffree. She says you lived in a sweet little house then.

**LILY DALE:**
Yes, over on Hawthorne.

**CLARA:**
She said your son was only a baby then.

**LILY DALE:**
Yes.

**CLARA:**
She said you may not remember her.

**LILY DALE:**
I remember her. She worked for us for almost three years. She must be quite up in years.

**CLARA:**
She is.

**LILY DALE:**
Who does she work for now?

**CLARA:**
She can't work now. Her health broke down.

**LILY DALE:**
Oh. I'm sorry to hear that.

**CLARA:**
She sent her regards to you.

**LILY DALE:**
And give mine to her.

**CLARA:**
She said you used to play such pretty music. She asked if you still played, and I said, no'm, she don't go near the piano. She read in the paper about your son dying. She said she was sorry. She remembers him, too, as a little boy. She says he was very lively and inquisitive.

**LILY DALE:**
Yes, he was.

*(A pause.)*

Is Mr. Will still in bed?

**CLARA:**
Yes ma'am.

**LILY DALE:**
Has he had his breakfast?

**CLARA:**
Yes ma'am. He had it early.

**LILY DALE:**
Did he have it in bed?

**CLARA:**
No ma'am, he ate in the breakfast room.

**LILY DALE:**
Where is Mr. Pete?

**CLARA:**
In his room.

**LILY DALE:**
Is his nephew with him?

**CLARA:**
Yes ma'am. Is he going to live here now?

**LILY DALE:**
Who?

**CLARA:**
Mr. Pete's nephew.

**LILY DALE:**
No, he just stayed last night.
*(A pause.)*
What's it like outside?

**CLARA:**
It's nice. Little cool.
*(PETE and CARSON enter.)*

**PETE:**
Good morning.

**LILY DALE:**
Good morning.

**CARSON:**
Good morning.

**PETE:**
Will not up?

**LILY DALE:**
Clara says he's been up and gone back to bed. How did you sleep?

**PETE:**
Not too well. Carson kept me up half the night telling me about my people back in Atlanta and what all happened to them. After he went to bed I spent the rest of the night practically thinking over what he told me.
*(A pause.)*
I think I may slip away for a few days, Lily Dale, if it's all right with you and Will, and go back to Atlanta with Carson. I think I want to see it one more time before I die.

**LILY DALE:**
When would you go?

**PETE:**
Today. We'll take the train, because I still have my pass.
Good morning, Clara.

**CLARA:**
Good morning. How about some breakfast?

**PETE:**
I'm not hungry. I just had a cup of coffee, but I know
Carson would like some. Wouldn't you, son?

**CARSON:**
Yes sir.
*(He leaves with CLARA.)*

**PETE:**
Did Will tell you what the doctor said?

**LILY DALE:**
No, Will is not talking to me still.

**PETE:**
He's told Will he doesn't think he can work for six months
or so.

**LILY DALE:**
Six months?

**PETE:**
That, of course, is quite a blow to Will. I feel so sorry for
him. I offered again to let him have the thirty-five thousand, at least twenty-five of it. I'm loaning Carson's sister

five thousand. We talked to her on the phone last night. She needs an operation. I guess her husband don't amount to much. He clerks in a supermarket in Atlanta. Carson is a fine young man, Lily Dale. He reminds me a lot of Bill. He had a high regard for Bill, you know. He said Bill had a wonderful education and was very smart. He said his one regret was that he had never had the opportunity to educate himself. I said it's never too late.

**LILY DALE:**
I thought you didn't believe in education, Pete.

**PETE:**
It's true I didn't use to. Of course, I had to get along without an education. I went to work at fourteen, so I only got to the seventh grade. And I thought I've done all right. I've made a living. I have no regrets. But I think today it's a different world. I think maybe you'd better get an education, if you can. Anyway, I told Carson that I'll help him along if he wants to go back to school. He says he'll pay me back, of course, when he finishes school and gets a job, and I know he will—he's a fine boy. I'd like him to go to school here, but he's got his heart set on the University of Georgia. Well, I said, if that's what you want.
*(WILL comes in.)*
Hello, young man.

**WILL:**
Good morning.

**PETE:**
I was telling Lily Dale I'm going away for a few days. Going to leave you two alone if it's all right with you.

**WILL:**
Where are you going?

**PETE:**
Atlanta. Look around and see what's left of my kin. I'll take the train. Like I told Lily Dale, that won't cost me anything but my meals, because I still have my pass. Carson says I can get a room cheap at that boardinghouse Bill used to stay in. Carson will stay with his sister. He'll sleep on the couch in the living room, as her bedrooms are all filled up with children. Two of them are not quite bright, but he says they have the disposition of saints. He'll watch out for them while his sister goes for her operation.
                    *(A pause.)*

**LILY DALE:**
Will, do you remember a maid we had while we lived on Hawthorne? Etta Doris Meneffree?

**WILL:**
No.

**LILY DALE:**
A good cook. Bill was five when she worked for us. He loved her so much.

**WILL:**
I don't remember her.

**PETE:**
I don't remember her either.
                    *(A pause.)*
We never had a cook the whole time I was married to your mama, even at the last when she got sick. She

wouldn't let us hire a cook. She'd force herself out of that bed no matter how bad she was feeling and fix my breakfast. She had to get up at four o'clock, too, because I had to be at work by five. I'd say, you don't feel well, stay in bed this morning, I can get my own breakfast, but she wouldn't have it. Up she'd get to fix me a big breakfast. The day she died she fixed my breakfast and when I came home that night I found her dead in the bed. And I went out in the kitchen to call you, Lily Dale, and there was my supper warming in the oven. She must have cooked it just before she died.

**WILL:**
Where is Carson?

**PETE:**
He's having his breakfast.

**WILL:**
Can he drive a car?

**PETE:**
I'm sure he can.

**WILL:**
I wonder if he would mind driving me downtown?

**LILY DALE:**
I don't think you should go downtown just yet, Will. I think—

**WILL:**
I'm going downtown. First Commerce Bank called.

**LILY DALE:**
Will!

**WILL:**
They want to talk to me about a loan. Pete, I am going to ask for that thirty-five thousand dollars now, so I can tell them how much cash I have on hand.

**PETE:**
Will, I'm sorry, but you told me you didn't want that money, and part of it I've promised now to Carson's sister. She needs an operation and—

**WILL:**
Oh, yes. I remember now your telling me something about that. I don't half listen these days. How much can I have?

**PETE:**
Well, I promised her five thousand and I promised Carson I'd loan him some money to get through college.
*(A pause.)*
And I was planning now on this trip to Atlanta.

**WILL:**
Never mind then.

**PETE:**
I can still let you have twenty-five thousand.

**WILL:**
Never mind. I'll bluff my way through someway. I'll—

**PETE:**
No, I want you to take the twenty-five thousand, Will. I'll feel terrible if you don't—please, Will.

**WILL:**
All right.

*(CARSON comes in.)*

**CARSON:**
I had a fine breakfast. Clara is a good cook.

**WILL:**
Can you drive, Carson?

**CARSON:**
Yes sir. I've been driving since I was fourteen. Never been able to afford a car of my own, though. Clara showed me the picture you had made up of Bill. It's a fine likeness. I just thought to myself, life is very strange. Here Bill and I were in the same town, in the same boardinghouse, and we were kin in a way and never ever knew it. My great-uncle was his step-grandfather. Isn't that something?

**WILL:**
Carson, can you drive me downtown?

**CARSON:**
Yes sir.

**WILL:**
I'm going to get dressed.

**PETE:**
Need any help?

**WILL:**
No thank you.

*(He goes.)*

## SCENE IV

**LILY DALE:**
Do you think I should call Will's doctor and tell him he's going downtown, Pete?

**PETE:**
I don't know, Lily Dale.

**LILY DALE:**
I'll go in the other room and call him. Excuse me.
*(She leaves.)*

**CARSON:**
Have you seen that picture they have of Bill?

**PETE:**
Yes.

**CARSON:**
Do you think it looks like him?

**PETE:**
Well, I believe it was taken some years ago.

**CARSON:**
I didn't want to say anything, but it doesn't look like the Bill I knew. He was very thin and stooped-shouldered and he was getting bald. Of course he was a great kidder. I used to say, you're well-named, because your name is Kidder. I like to go to picture shows, and every night he'd ask me where I was off to and before I could answer he'd say, I know, don't tell me—the picture show. His roommate liked picture shows too. But Bill never would go. He would just stay in their room and read.
*(LILY DALE comes back in.)*

**LILY DALE:**
The doctor says he shouldn't go. He should stay in his bed and rest for at least two more weeks. Will you tell him that, Pete?

**PETE:**
You tell it to him, Lily Dale.

**CARSON:**
I met Bill's roommate at the YMCA yesterday. He said he'd seen me out here when he came by the other day. He asked how I know you all and I told him I was kin in a way and he said did I know why you all had turned against him and—
*(WILL comes in. He is dressed.)*

**WILL:**
Let's go, Carson.

**CARSON:**
Yes sir.
*(He and WILL start out.)*

**LILY DALE:**
Will. I called your doctor. He said you shouldn't go, not for two weeks. He said you must stay in bed and rest.

**WILL:**
The hell with the doctor. I'm going. Come on, Carson.

**CARSON:**
Yes sir.
*(They leave.)*

**PETE:**

I think he's going to be all right, Lily Dale. It may be the best thing for him. Particularly if it's good news. That will cheer him up and give him something to think about.

*(CLARA comes in.)*

**CLARA:**

Miss Lily Dale, Etta Doris is in the kitchen. She says she would like to say hello to you. Can I bring her in?

**LILY DALE:**

All right.

*(CLARA goes.)*

She's a cook that used to work for us. I told you about her earlier. You didn't remember her.

**PETE:**

Oh, yes.

*(CLARA and ETTA DORIS enter.)*

**ETTA DORIS:**

Oh. I don't believe it. She ain't changed at all. Not one pound heavier, and look at me—wore out. Wore out cookin' in other people's kitchens. She ain't changed.

**LILY DALE:**

Oh, I have too changed, Etta Doris.

**ETTA DORIS:**

No, not a day. How long has it been, Miss Lily Dale?

**LILY DALE:**

Oh, heavens. Too long.

**ETTA DORIS:**
An' this your husband. Mr. Will, as I remember.

**LILY DALE:**
No, he's not my husband—he's my stepfather.

**ETTA DORIS:**
Oh, yes. How do you do? You're a fine-lookin' man, so young-lookin' to be her stepfather. Your mama has passed, Clara told me.

**LILY DALE:**
Yes. Ten years ago.

**ETTA DORIS:**
Ten years ago. Mercy. Everything changes. The Lord giveth and he taketh away. And your boy—I was heartsick to hear about it. He drowned.

**LILY DALE:**
Yes.

**ETTA DORIS:**
Mercy. Mercy. We're here today and gone tomorrow. Blessed be the name of the Lord. An' you don't play no more on the piano, Clara tells me.

**LILY DALE:**
No, not since my boy died.

**CLARA:**
She's very religious. She prays all the time.

**ETTA DORIS:**
Bless your heart. Pray for me, honey.

**LILY DALE:**
I will.

**ETTA DORIS:**
And how is your husband?

**LILY DALE:**
He's all right, thank you.

**ETTA DORIS:**
Clara says he had a little spell with his heart.

**LILY DALE:**
Yes.

**ETTA DORIS:**
Well, give my regards to him.

**LILY DALE:**
I will.

**ETTA DORIS:**
I'll be going now. I just took a chance on you being here.

**LILY DALE:**
Thank you for coming by.

**ETTA DORIS:**
Yes ma'am.
            *(ETTA DORIS and CLARA leave.)*

**LILY DALE:**
What time will you leave, Pete?

**PETE:**
Four.

**LILY DALE:**
How long will you stay?

**PETE:**
Two or three days. I have a phone number where I can be reached in case you need me.

**LILY DALE:**
All right.

**PETE:**
I'm going to pack.

**LILY DALE:**
All right, Pete. (*He goes.*)
                    (*Calling:*)
Clara!
            (*CLARA enters.*)

**CLARA:**
Yes ma'am.

**LILY DALE:**
Is Etta Doris still here?

**CLARA:**
Yes ma'am. I'm fixing her a sandwich. I hope you don't mind.

**LILY DALE:**
No, I don't mind. How did she get here? Does she have a car?

**CLARA:**
No'm. She took a bus. She still had to walk four blocks.
She said she was just determined to get a look at you
again.

**LILY DALE:**
Ask her if she's ever heard of Disappointment Clubs here
in Houston.

**CLARA:**
Yes ma'am.
                    *(She starts out.)*

**LILY DALE:**
And did you ask your friend Lucille if she knew if Mrs.
Roosevelt had anything to do with the Disappointment
Clubs?

**CLARA:**
I forgot, but I will ask her.
                    *(She goes. PETE enters.)*

**PETE:**
All packed.

**LILY DALE:**
So soon?

**PETE:**
I'm not taking much. I don't have much to take, to tell
you the truth.

**LILY DALE:**
I think I'm going downtown for a while, Pete. I have been
in the house so much.

**PETE:**
I think that's a good idea.

**LILY DALE:**
If you're gone before I get back, have a wonderful time and let us hear when you get there.

**PETE:**
I will.

> *(CLARA comes in.)*

**CLARA:**
She never heard of the Disappointment Club either.

**LILY DALE:**
Oh. Thank you, Clara.

> *(CLARA starts away.)*

Clara, I'm going downtown for a while. When Mr. Will gets back, tell him I'll be here in plenty of time for supper.

**CLARA:**
Yes ma'am.

> *(She goes.)*

**LILY DALE:**
Goodbye, Pete.

**PETE:**
Goodbye.

> *(He kisses her. She leaves as the lights fade.)*

# ❦ SCENE V ❦

*Mid-afternoon. PETE is in the den. CARSON and WILL enter.*

**PETE:**
Well, I was getting a little worried about you two.

**CARSON:**
I picked up my clothes at the YMCA.

**PETE:**
Well, we still got plenty of time. How did it go, Will?

**WILL:**
Nothing happened. It was just a courtesy call.

**PETE:**
Who did you talk to? Anyone you've known before?

**WILL:**

A boy younger than Carson. I bet he wasn't more than twenty-five.


**PETE:**

Was he polite?


**WILL:**

Oh, yeah. He was polite. But that's about all. He said what he had to tell me, he didn't want to tell me over the phone, as he wanted me to understand they had a real interest in me and valued me as a customer and hoped one day to do business with me, but he had to be candid and say this was not, in his opinion, the best time to start a new business, but not to be discouraged and to come back if I hadn't found another bank interested in six months and perhaps the climate would have changed by then and I said, do you know you got me out of a sickbed to tell me this?, and he began again about how he felt the telephone was too unpersonal and he personally wanted to meet me, and make me feel they were interested in me, and then when I left him I ran into Ted Cleveland Jr. He said he'd heard I'd been sick and he was sorry and I thanked him and he said, did you get my get-well card, and I said I had and he said, we might be able to find something for you with less responsibility down at the company, did Tom tell you that, and I said he had and I said—

*(A pause.)*

I can't believe what I said.

*(A pause.)*

I said, I appreciate your thinking of me and maybe when I'm stronger I'll be around and talk to you about it. And he said, well, in the meantime don't be a stranger, and I said no, I wouldn't be.

*(A pause.)*

Did you eat lunch?

**PETE:**
Not yet.

**WILL:**
Where is Lily Dale?

**PETE:**
She went downtown.

**WILL:**
Are you and Carson hungry?

**PETE:**
I'm hungry. How about you, Carson?

**CARSON:**
I can always eat.

**WILL** *(calling)*:
Clara!

*(A pause.)*

What did Lily Dale go to town for?

**PETE:**
She didn't say.

**WILL:**
She probably went over to the YMCA to give money to
that boy.

**PETE:**
Now, Will.

**WILL:**

I know. I've been mean as hell to her, and I'm sorry. I just haven't felt well, and that tends to make you mean, I guess.

*(CLARA comes in.)*

How about some lunch, Clara?

**CLARA:**

Sure. It's all there waiting. You all ready?

**WILL:**

I'm not eating, you all go on.

**PETE:**

You have to eat, Will.

**WILL:**

I'll eat later. I want to rest now. I can't believe I thanked Ted Cleveland Jr. for offering me a lousy job.

**PETE:**

It may not be a lousy job, Will.

**WILL:**

It's one I'll never take. I'll go on relief first.

**PETE:**

Don't say that, Will.

**WILL:**

I'm just ranting and raving. Go eat your lunch.

**PETE:**

Come on, Carson.

*(They go. WILL lies down on the sofa. He closes his*

*eyes. CLARA comes in, followed by ETTA DORIS, who waits by the door.)*

**CLARA:**
Mr. Will, excuse me for disturbing you, but Etta Doris used to work for you all and she wanted to say hello to you before she goes.
*(WILL gets up from the couch.)*

**WILL:**
Bring her in.
*(ETTA DORIS comes over to WILL.)*

**ETTA DORIS:**
Do you remember me?

**WILL:**
No, I can't say I do. I'm sorry.

**ETTA DORIS:**
I remember you well. You were crazy about baseball. You used to come in every day after work and say, I'm on my way to baseball practice.

**WILL:**
I sure did. That is right. I certainly did.

**ETTA DORIS:**
You must be prospering, living in a fine house like this.

**WILL:**
We get along.

**ETTA DORIS:**
I hear you been poorly. I'm poorly all the time. It's your heart?

**WILL:**
Yes.

**ETTA DORIS:**
I got all kind of things wrong with me. High blood pressure, arthritis, lower back pains. I can't work at all no more. I'm on the old age. You get your old age yet?

**WILL:**
No, not yet.

**ETTA DORIS:**
I went last week to try to find that house you all lived in when I worked for you. It's gone.

**WILL:**
Yes, it was torn down a while back.

**ETTA DORIS:**
They're tearing down everything in Houston, seems like to me.

**WILL:**
It seems like it. You'll have to excuse me now, I'm feeling tired.

**ETTA DORIS:**
Yes sir.

**WILL:**
Nice to see you again.

**ETTA DORIS:**
Yes sir. I was sorry about your boy.

**WILL:**
Thank you.

**ETTA DORIS:**
You were bound and determined to make him a baseball player, too. Did he take to it?

**WILL:**
No, he never did.

**ETTA DORIS:**
Well, I declare. He was a sweet boy. Blond, blue-eyed.

**WILL:**
Yes.

**ETTA DORIS:**
Pretty.

**WILL:**
Yes.

**ETTA DORIS:**
And the friendliest little boy I ever saw. Never knew a stranger.

**WILL:**
Yes, he was very friendly.

**ETTA DORIS:**
Did he keep on that way?

**WILL:**

I think so. More or less.

**ETTA DORIS:**

I went back to see your wife a year or two after I had stopped working for you all and he had just come in from school. She said he was smart. Made good grades.

**WILL:**

Yes, he was.

**ETTA DORIS:**

And I said to him, you remember me, little boy? Yes, ma'am, he said. I remember you well.

> *(She laughs.)*

That's what he said. I remember you well.

> *(A pause.)*

That was a long time ago. I'm sorry I never got to see him again.

> *(She and* CLARA *go.* WILL *is left alone. He goes to the phone. He dials.)*

**WILL:**

Tom, this is Will Kidder. . . . Pretty fair. Look, I hope you didn't tell Ted about our conversation, because I've been thinking it over and maybe when I'm stronger I will come in and talk to him. Do you have any idea what he has in mind? . . . Oh, I see. All right. . . . Yeah. I'll see you soon.

*(He hangs up the phone.* CARSON *and* PETE *come in.)*

**PETE:**

We're on our way. I'll call you from Atlanta.

**WILL:**

Fine, Pete.

**CARSON:**
So long, sir.

**WILL:**
Are we going to be seeing you again, Carson?

**CARSON:**
Might be.

**WILL:**
I hope so. Good luck to you.

**CARSON:**
Thank you. Good luck to you.
> *(WILL starts out of the room. He pauses.)*

**WILL:**
Carson, would you help me back to my room, son? I feel kind of weak.

**PETE:**
Maybe we shouldn't leave until Lily Dale gets here.

**WILL:**
No, I'll be fine once I get on the bed.

**PETE:**
I still think—

**WILL:**
Go on now. Clara is here if I need anything.
> *(He and CARSON continue out of the room as the
> lights fade.)*

# ❧ SCENE VI ❧

*The lights are brought up on the den. It is later the same day. LILY DALE is there. CLARA comes in.*

**CLARA:**
Oh, Miss Lily Dale, you're back. I asked my friend Lucille if Mrs. Roosevelt had anything to do with the Disappointment Clubs and she said not that she ever heard of. She said Mrs. Roosevelt was in Houston once, though. She'd seen her. Got as close to her as I am to you. She said she was a fine lady.

**LILY DALE:**
I'm sure. How's Will?

**CLARA:**
He's resting. Mr. Pete and his nephew left for Atlanta. They're thick as thieves.

**LILY DALE:**
Yes, they are.

*(A pause.)*

Clara.

**CLARA:**
Yes, ma'am.

**LILY DALE:**
I've done a terrible thing.

**CLARA:**
What you done?

**LILY DALE:**
I've seen that young man again.

**CLARA:**
Mr. Bill's friend?

**LILY DALE:**
Yes. He was standing in the drive when I pulled out my car and I had to stop or I would have run over him and he came to the car and asked me what had happened to turn me against him, and I said, get in the car. It seemed we drove all over Houston, and I told him everything that Pete's nephew had told Pete and he said he was a liar and he had made the whole thing up because he was jealous of him and I said why was he jealous of him and he said, because I was Bill's friend and he wasn't. He said, if I'm so terrible why did he try to get me to room with him at the YMCA, and I said, did you room with him, and he said, no, I wouldn't be caught dead in the same room with him, and I said, you do have a mother and a sister, and he said, oh yes, a precious mother and a precious sister, and I said,

what about Bill's praying, Pete's nephew said you made that up, and he is a liar, he said, ask anybody back in the boardinghouse who tells lies and who tells the truth, he says Pete's nephew is known as a notorious liar all over Atlanta.

**CLARA:**
You don't say. Where is that young man now?

**LILY:**
He's hiding out there. In my car. I'm going to try and get Will to speak to him.
(*WILL comes in, again in pajamas and robe.*)

**WILL:**
Where have you been?

**LILY DALE:**
Just downtown. I did a little window shopping.

**WILL:**
You better not buy anything for a while now.

**LILY DALE:**
I know, Will.

**WILL:**
We have a lot of bills.

**LILY DALE:**
I know, Will. How did it go at the bank?

**WILL:**
Not too well. It was just a courtesy thing.
(*A pause.*)

I've lost my spirit, Lily Dale. I know I've been cross with you, and I'm sorry. But I have to tell you I am worried. I've just lost my spirit.

**LILY DALE:**
Please, please don't keep saying that, honey.

**WILL:**
For the first time in my life I don't know where to turn or what to do. Here I am in the finest city in the greatest country in the world and I don't know where to turn. I'm whipped. I'm whipped.

**LILY DALE:**
Will, please.

**WILL:**
I'm not mad at you anymore, Lily Dale.

**LILY DALE:**
I'm glad of that, Daddy.

**WILL:**
But please answer me this one thing.
                    *(He sees CLARA.)*
Clara, would you mind leaving us alone?

**CLARA:**
No sir.

                    *(She goes.)*

**WILL:**
Why did you give that boy money, Lily Dale? Behind my back after I had asked you not to see him again or go near him? Didn't I ask you that?

**LILY DALE:**
Yes, you did.

**WILL:**
Then why, Lily Dale? Why?

**LILY DALE:**
I don't know. I felt sorry for him. He had a sick mother, he lost his job, his sister was deserted with three small children.

**WILL:**
All lies, as we know now. But even if they were true, after I had asked you—

**LILY DALE:**
I know. I know. I have never deceived you before, Daddy, except for one time. It was when you went to Chicago for a business trip and my cousin Mary Cunningham came to stay with me and she talked me into letting two men come over to the house. And you came back from Chicago unexpectedly and they ran out of the back door.
*(A pause.)*
That was twenty years ago. I don't know why I had to tell you that. It has bothered me all these years—not that I would have done anything wrong. . . .
*(A pause.)*
I get lonely, Will. You've always had your work, gone away so much of the time, and then Bill went off to school, and then of course I had my music, but when Bill died I couldn't go near the piano anymore and I decided I should dedicate myself to God, and then this young friend of Bill's comes and he was sweet to me, and I missed Bill so, and I would always talk to him about Bill. And I never told you this, but just before Alice Temple committed suicide I

went to see her and she told me that Bill had committed suicide, that everyone said that, and it upset me so, and I didn't want to tell you because I was afraid it would upset you, so I called his sweet friend in Atlanta and he told me he did not because he had talked to him the night before and all he talked about was God.

**WILL:**
That boy is a liar, Lily Dale.

**LILY DALE:**
He may be, Will, but it did comfort me to hear him say it, and I needed comforting, Will. I've spent my days here crying since Bill died, and I wouldn't have done anything in the world to hurt you, Will, because you know how much I love you and how grateful I am for all you've given me, and I do believe in prayer, Will, and I'm going to pray that you get well and strong and you'll find a way to start your business.

**WILL:**
Bill did kill himself, Lily Dale.

**LILY DALE:**
Don't say that, Will.

**WILL:**
I'm sorry, but I think he did.

**LILY DALE:**
You think? But you don't know. What a terrible thing to say about your son!

**WILL:**
Why did he come swimming in the middle of the afternoon

in the lake in Florida and walk and continue to walk until
he got water over his head? Why? Lily Dale, why?
*(A pause.)*
Lily, Lily Dale, why? I failed him, Lily Dale. Some way I
failed him. I tried to be a good father, but I just think now
I only wanted him to be like me, I never tried to understand what he was like. I never tried to find out what he
would want to do, what he would want to talk about. Life
goes so fast, Lily Dale. My God. It goes so fast. It seems
like yesterday he was a baby, and I was holding him in
my arms, and before I turned around good he was off to
school and I thought, when he comes back he'll come into
the business and I'll be close to him.
*(A pause.)*
I was never close to him, Lily Dale. How was your day?
Fine, son, how was yours? And then he was gone.
*(A pause.)*
I want my son back, Lily Dale. I want him back.
*(A pause.)*


**LILY DALE:**
I know. I know. So do I.
*(A pause.)*
I have to tell you this one last thing, Will. I saw Bill's friend
today. He stood in the driveway as I was backing the car
out and if I hadn't stopped I would have run over him,
and he came to the car and I told him what Carson said
and he said Carson was the liar—that—
*(WILL has closed his eyes.)*
He said that Carson was jealous of his friendship with Bill
and. . . .
*(A pause.)*
Will, I haven't told you the whole truth about those two
men that came to the house with me and Mary Cunningham. They didn't come to our house because Mary invited

them. We were riding down Main Street in Mary's car and these two men passed us slowly in their car and looked back at us, and Mary said, they want to flirt, let's flirt back. Well, Mary, I said, I'm a married woman, Will wouldn't like that. What Will doesn't know won't hurt him, she said— besides, flirting is harmless, so she stepped on the gas and passed those men and looked back in this bold kind of way and as she did so, they stepped on the gas and drove right up beside us and introduced themselves, and Mary before I could stop her told them her name and my name and they told us theirs and they asked us to go to their apartment and Mary said we weren't that kind of girl and they said they meant no harm by it, as they just wanted to go someplace where we could talk and get to know each other, and then without asking my permission she said we could all go to my house and gave them the address.

*(A pause.)*

And do you know why I've stopped seeing Mary Cunningham? She said that one time when she was visiting Mama and Pete in Houston, Pete tried to put his arm around her and kiss her when Mama went out of the room. I said, I do not believe a word of that, and she said the same thing happened to our cousin Mabel Thornton when she was visiting them, and their mama wouldn't allow them to stay at Mama's any longer after that. Do you believe that?

**WILL:**

I don't know. Who knows about anything, Lily Dale? I'm just very tired, that's all I know. Just very tired. Very, very tired.

**LILY DALE:**

Who are we to believe, Daddy? Pete's great-nephew Carson, or Bill's friend? Bill's friend asked if you would

please see him and let him tell you what he told me. He says he is not a liar, that every word he has said to us is the truth. That Bill was very religious and he did pray loud and clear so that everybody in the boardinghouse could hear him, he said, and he cried as he was telling me.
*(A pause.)*
I feel so sorry for him, Daddy. He's not able to find work and he is alone here in Houston. . . .
*(A pause.)*

**WILL:**
I ran into Ted Jr. at the bank, Lily Dale. He said they would like to find something for me to do at the company again, and I wanted to say, Go stuff it, but I didn't. I thanked him, and I have to tell you I may have to swallow my pride and go back there and see what they'll dole out to me.

**LILY DALE:**
Whatever you think best, Will. And you know what I've been thinking—maybe I could start teaching music and that would help us out, too.

**WILL:**
If you like. It might give you something to think about.
*(A pause.)*

**LILY DALE:**
Will?

**WILL:**
Yes?
*(He takes her hand.)*
We're going to make it, Lily Dale. We always have.

**LILY DALE:**
I know.

*(A pause.)*

Will?

**WILL:**
Yes.

**LILY DALE:**
Would you do me one last favor?

**WILL:**
What is it?

**LILY DALE:**
Would you speak to Bill's friend? Let him tell you his side of the story. That is all he asks. Then he says he'll go away and leave us alone forever if you want him to. Would you see him, Will? He's outside in my car.

**WILL:**
No.

**LILY DALE:**
Will.

**WILL:**
No.

**LILY DALE:**
Why, Will? Why can't you just talk to him?

**WILL:**
Because I don't want to, Lily Dale. Because there are

things I'd have to ask him and I don't want to know the answers.

**LILY DALE:**
Like what?

**WILL:**
You know the money I gave Bill at Christmas?

**LILY DALE:**
Yes, and that he spent.

**WILL:**
And I told you I didn't know how he spent it. Well, I didn't tell you the truth. In his safety box there were some canceled checks totaling a hundred thousand dollars and they were all made out to his friend.

**LILY DALE:**
Will, maybe there was a reason.

**WILL:**
Maybe so. But I don't want to know what it is. Ever. So tell him that for me. That I know my son gave him a hundred thousand dollars and maybe it was for his sick mother, too, or his sister, but I don't believe it. And I don't believe—anyway, whatever the reasons, I don't want to know. There was a Bill I knew and a Bill you knew and that's the only Bill I care to know about.

**LILY DALE:**
What will I tell him?

**WILL:**
Just tell him to please go away and leave us alone.

**LILY DALE:**
All right, Will.
*(She goes. WILL goes to the phone. He dials.)*

**WILL:**
Tom? . . . How about my coming in tomorrow? . . . Early afternoon—all right. I'll be there. Thank you.
*(He hangs up the phone. LILY DALE comes in.)*

**LILY DALE:**
I told him, Will. He cried, Will, when I told him. He said Bill insisted on giving him the money, for buying nice things. He said he was like a father to him and he'd never known his father, and that—and he'd go back to Atlanta now and not bother us anymore and he was sorry if he had upset us in any way. He is a sweet boy, Will, I don't care what anybody says.
*(A pause.)*
He said, too, that he wished he could have gone down in the water that day with Bill. That's how much he loved him and missed him.
*(She's crying.)*
Oh my God, Will, oh my God.

**WILL:**
Don't cry, Lily Dale. Everything is going to be all right. If I go back to work and you start teaching, everything will be all right.
*(He holds her as the lights fade.)*

Ⓟ PLUME

# GREAT THEATER

- ☐ **M. BUTTERFLY by David Henry Hwang. With an Afterword by the playwright.** 1988 Tony Award-Winner for Best Play and now a major motion picture from Warner Bros. "A many-splendored theatrical treasure. A thrilling drama. A sensational real-life story of love and treachery."—Frederick Winship, *United Press International* (272599—$9.00)

- ☐ **THE KENTUCKY CYCLE by Robert Schenkkan.** In this series of nine short plays, Pulitzer Prize-winning playwright Robert Schenkkan has created a mesmerizing epic saga of rural Kentucky—an unblinking look at the truth behind our American mythology, and at the men and women who founded this country. "Aspires to nothing less than the history of the U.S. . . . strives for mythic power—and attains it."—*Time* (269679—$14.95)

- ☐ **THE DESTINY OF ME A Play by Larry Kramer author of** *The Normal Heart*. Funny, gutsy, and unabashedly emotional . . . has the power to hit us where it hurts—in the heart. AIDS activist Ned Weeks, frightened of dying of the disease . . . checks himself into an experimental treatment program run by the very doctor that his militant organization has been criticizing most. "Overwhelmingly powerful."—Frank Rich, *The New York Times* (270162—$9.95)

- ☐ **JEFFREY by Paul Rudnick.** "The hottest ticket off-Broadway . . . Even with AIDS lurking in the background, *Jeffrey* sparkles. Mr. Rudnick . . . has come up with some of the funniest lines and deftest gimmicks onstage today. [He] is a master of one-liners."—*Wall Street Journal* (276144—$7.95)

- ☐ **LATER LIFE** *And Two Other Plays:* **The Old Boy** *and* **The Snow Ball. by A.R. Gurney.** This collection of three plays brings us incomparable Gurney—mature, masterful, and hilarious. All three works skillfully juxtapose conflicting emotions to blend wit and sadness, self-realization with self-delusion, and barren interior lives with the façade of prosperous middle-class existences. "There's no dramatist like him on either side of the Atlantic."—*The New Yorker* (272513—$10.95)

Prices slightly higher in Canada.

---

Visa and Mastercard holders can order Plume, Meridian, and Dutton books by calling
**1-800-253-6476.**
They are also available at your local bookstore. Allow 4-6 weeks for delivery.
This offer is subject to change without notice.

Ⓟ **PLUME**
 **DUTTON**

# CENTER STAGE

☐ **MASTER CLASS by Terrence McNally.** Inspired by a series of master classes the great diva conducted at Juilliard toward the end of her career, this drama puts Maria Callas at center stage again as she coaxes, prods, and inspires students—"victims" she calls them—into giving the performances of their lives while revealing her own. As she slips off into memories, we experience her days at La Scala, her marriage to Meneghini, and her great doomed love for Aristotle Onassis. "A play of notable wit, humanity and insight . . . captures the transcendent experience. You share, for a moment, in the making of art."—*Philadelphia Inquirer* (276152—$8.95)

☐ **SHADOWLANDS by William Nicholson.** This extraordinary play based on the true story of the British philosopher and highly successful author of children's fantasies, C.S. Lewis, brilliantly portrays how love profoundly alters the idealistic philosopher—more than any teacher, book, or thought had before. "Engrossing, entertaining . . . literate, well-crafted, and discreetly brilliant." —Clive Barnes, *New York Post* (267323—$7.95)

☐ **LOVE LETTERS And Two Other Plays:** *The Golden Age* and *What I Did Last Summer.* **by A.R. Gurney.** In *Love Letters* the author has captured the manners of upper-middle-class WASP America. Tracing the lifelong correspondence of the staid, dutiful lawyer Andrew Makepeace Ladd III and the lively, unstable artist Melissa Gardner, the story of their bittersweet relationship gradually unfolds from what is written—and what is left unsaid—in their letters. Two other plays are also included here, providing a trio of wry and affectionate paeans to love lost, found, and fleetingly glimpsed. (265010—$10.95)

Prices slightly higher in Canada.

---

Visa and Mastercard holders can order Plume, Meridian, and Dutton books by calling
**1-800-253-6476.**
They are also available at your local bookstore. Allow 4-6 weeks for delivery.
This offer is subject to change without notice.